Home Safety

by Sheila Rivera

first step nonfiction

ᘰ Lerner Publications Company · Minneapolis

How do I stay safe at home?

I lock the door.

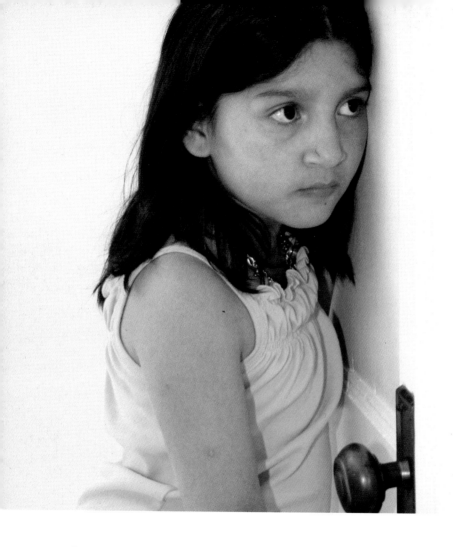

I do not let strangers inside.

I stay away from poisons.

I do not play with knives.

I do not take medicine
without an adult.

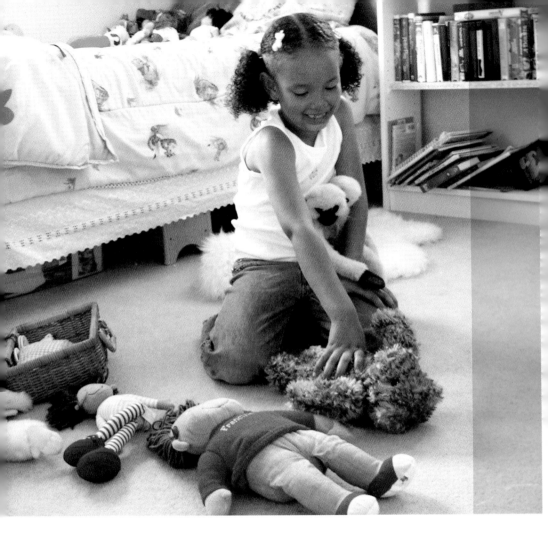

I pick up my toys so
nobody trips.